*IMPRESSIONS of*

# EXMOOR & DARTMOOR

Produced by AA Publishing
© AA Media Limited 2009

Published by AA Publishing (a trading name of AA Media Limited, whose registered
office is Fanum House, Basing View,
Basingstoke, Hampshire RG21 4EA; registered number 06112600)

ISBN: 978-0-7495-6178-9
A04091

A CIP catalogue record for this book is available from the British Library.

Colour reproduction by KDP, Kingsclere
Printed and bound in China by C & C Offset Printing Co. Ltd

*Opposite: A Dartmoor pony mare with its foal at Haytor, Dartmoor National Park.*

# IMPRESSIONS *of*

# EXMOOR & DARTMOOR

Picture Acknowledgements

The Automobile Association wishes to thank the following photographers and organisations
for their assistance in the preparation of this book.

Abbreviations for the picture credits are as follows – (AA) AA World Travel Library

3 AA/Nigel Hicks; 5 AA/Roger Moss; 7 AA/Guy Edwardes; 8 AA/Nigel Hicks; 9 AA/Wyn Voysey; 10 AA/Peter Baker;
11 AA/Steve Day; 12 AA/Caroline Jones; 13 AA/Nigel Hicks; 14 AA/Nigel Hicks; 15 AA/Roger Moss; 16 AA/Caroline
Jones; 17 AA/Nigel Hicks; 18 AA/Nigel Hicks; 19 AA/Nigel Hicks; 20 AA/Caroline Jones; 21 AA/Nigel Hicks;
22 AA/Nigel Hicks; 23 AA/Caroline Jones; 24 AA/Caroline Jones; 25 AA/Nigel Hicks; 26 AA/Nigel Hicks;
27 AA/Caroline Jones; 28 AA/Caroline Jones; 29 AA/Nigel Hicks; 30 AA/Nigel Hicks; 31 AA/Nigel Hicks;
32 AA/Nigel Hicks; 33 AA/Caroline Jones; 34 AA/Nigel Hicks; 35 AA/Nigel Hicks; 36 AA/Nigel Hicks; 37 AA/Nigel
Hicks; 38 AA/Nigel Hicks; 39 AA/Nigel Hicks; 40 AA/Nigel Hicks; 41 AA/Nigel Hicks; 42 AA/Nigel Hicks;
43 AA/Nigel Hicks; 44 AA/Nigel Hicks; 45 AA/Nigel Hicks; 46 AA/Nigel Hicks; 47 AA/Nigel Hicks; 48 AA/Nigel
Hicks; 49 AA/Guy Edwardes; 50 AA/Guy Edwardes; 51 AA/Nigel Hicks; 52 AA/Nigel Hicks; 53 AA/Nigel Hicks;
54 AA/Nigel Hicks; 55 AA/Nigel Hicks; 56 AA/Guy Edwardes; 57 AA/Guy Edwardes; 58 AA/Guy Edwardes;
59 AA/Guy Edwardes; 60 AA/Guy Edwardes; 61 AA/Guy Edwardes; 62 AA/Nigel Hicks; 63 AA/Nigel Hicks;
64 AA/Nigel Hicks; 65 AA/Nigel Hicks; 66 AA/Nigel Hicks; 67 AA/Nigel Hicks; 68 AA/Nigel Hicks; 69 AA/Nigel
Hicks; 70 AA/Guy Edwardes; 71 AA/Guy Edwardes; 72 AA/Guy Edwardes; 73 AA/Guy Edwardes; 74 AA/Guy
Edwardes; 75 AA/Nigel Hicks; 76 AA/Nigel Hicks; 77 AA/Harry Williams; 78 AA/Nigel Hicks; 79 AA/Guy Edwardes;
80 AA/Guy Edwardes; 81 AA/Guy Edwardes; 82 AA/Guy Edwardes; 83 AA/Nigel Hicks; 84 AA/Nigel Hicks;
85 AA/Guy Edwardes; 86 AA/Caroline Jones; 87 AA/Guy Edwardes; 88 AA/Guy Edwardes; 89 AA/Guy Edwardes;
90 AA/Guy Edwardes; 91 AA/Guy Edwardes; 92 AA/Guy Edwardes; 93 AA/Guy Edwardes; 94 AA/Nigel Hicks;
95 AA/Neil Setchfield.

Every effort has been made to trace the copyright holders, and we apologise in advance for any accidental errors. We
would be happy to apply any corrections in the following edition of this publication.

*Opposite: The trees, fields and hills of Exmoor, seen from Withypool, Exmoor National Park.*

# INTRODUCTION

Exmoor National Park is a protected area, granted National Park status in 1954 to help conserve its outstanding natural beauty and wildlife. Its five National Park Visitor Centres are located at Dunster, Lynmouth, Combe Martin, County Gate and Dulverton. Straddling the Devon-Somerset border (two-thirds of the moor falls in Somerset), Exmoor's main attractions are its stunning coastline running along beneath England's highest, most spectacular sea-cliffs. There are few sandy beaches, but glorious expanses can be found at Woolacombe and Saunton Sands.

Exmoor is home to a diversity of wildlife including the native Exmoor pony, wild red deer, buzzards and foxes. The high heather moorland, wooded gorges, waterfalls, ancient oak woodland, valleys and combes attract those in search of clean air and tranquillity - it is possible to walk for miles across Exmoor and not see another person. Although Exmoor is hilly, it offers great cycling: its terrain presents challenge and enjoyment to road cyclists and mountain bikers. Horseriding is also a very popular way to explore the beautiful National Park, with over 400 miles of well-maintained bridle paths threading their way through its environs.

Many historic houses and gardens can be found within Exmoor National Park. These grand places include the Regency Arlington Court to the south of Combe Martin, the Victorian country house of Knightshayes Court, near Dulverton, and romantic Dunster Castle, with its fine interior and subtropical gardens. Other popular places to visit include Tarr Steps (the largest clapper bridge in Britain) and the Church of St Beuno at Culbone, which can only be reached on foot and is reputedly the smallest church in Britain.

The tough, somewhat bleak moorland expanse of Dartmoor became a National Park in 1951. It is famed for its solitude and majesty; a place of vast wild spaces where nature is quick to reclaim parts of the landscape previously scarred by man, such as Haytor Granite Quarry. Within the confines of the National Park, the largest and highest upland in southern Britain, you can discover granite tors and lowland heaths, blanket bogs and upland oakwoods, all grazed by the famous hardy breed of Dartmoor pony.

The area also has a softer, prettier side, with many charming pubs and restaurants serving local ales and traditional Devon fayre, tempting visitors to indulge in delicious Devon cream teas with freshly baked scones, jam and clotted cream. Among the picturebook villages of Dartmoor you will find craft shops selling traditional hand-made fudge, rustic pottery and works of art. Those who like to commune with nature will find Dartmoor's clean and sparkling rivers teeming with wild brown trout, sea trout and salmon. The area's many well-known landmarks include the Tavistock Canal, High Willhays (the highest point in Dartmoor), the ancient burial site of Childe's Tomb, the strange rock formation of Bowerman's Nose and the Bronze Age stone circle of Grey Wethers, all of which demand exploration on foot, bike or pony.

*Opposite: Scorhill Stone Circle at sunset near the village of Chagford in Dartmoor National Park.*

*Becky Falls, near Manaton, Dartmoor National Park.*

*The River Barle runs through Dulverton and is fronted by quaint cottages on the side of the wooded Barle Valley, Exmoor National Park.*

*A shop full of interesting curios and old furniture in Church Street, Dunster, Exmoor National Park.*

*Exmoor National Park seen from Dunkery Beacon, the highest point on Exmoor.*

*Colourful heather and gorse at Haytor Rocks, Dartmoor National Park.*

*A sundew growing in a bog near Widecombe in the Moor, Dartmoor National Park.*

*Foxton Mires, marshland and source of the River Dart, near Princetown, Dartmoor National Park.*

*Dunster's Norman castle, which dominates the village from its hilltop location, has been substantially altered throughout its history, although it is now in the care of the National Trust.*

*The Cliff Railway at Lynmouth, Exmoor National Park.*

*Cotton grass growing in Foxton Mires, marshland and source of the River Dart, near Princetown, Dartmoor National Park.*

*The administrative building at Buckfast Abbey, Buckfastleigh, Dartmoor National Park.*
*Opposite: The ruins of Okehampton Castle, Okehampton, Dartmoor National Park.*

*The pretty town of Lynmouth, Exmoor National Park.*

*Buckfast Abbey, Buckfastleigh, Dartmoor National Park.*

*Calves at play in the early morning sunlight on Haytor, Dartmoor National Park.*

*Boats in the harbour at Lynmouth, Exmoor National Park.*

*Another view of Lynmouth's stone-built harbour, Exmoor National Park.*

*The River Dart flowing briskly through the Dart Valley Nature Reserve, New Bridge, Dartmoor National Park.*

*A window in the ruined chapel, Okehampton Castle, Dartmoor National Park.*

*The rooftops of Lynton, Exmoor National Park.*

*Valley of the Rocks, Lynton, Exmoor National Park.*

*A Dartmoor pony mare and its foal at Haytor, Dartmoor National Park.*

*The River Dart flowing round and over rocks at Dartmeet, Dartmoor National Park.*

*Bluebells in flower on Hound Tor, Dartmoor National Park.*

*Bluebells growing near Hound Tor, which is just visible in the background, Dartmoor National Park.*

*Castle Rock in the Valley of the Rocks, Exmoor National Park.*

*A group of anglers fishing in Porlock Bay, seen from Hurlstone Point, Exmoor National Park.*

*Roses growing up a cottage wall, Bossington, near Porlock, Exmoor National Park.*

*The pebble beach and wooded coastline near Porlock, Exmoor National Park.*

*A hawthorn tree in flower near Dartmeet, Dartmoor National Park.*

*Haytor seen in early morning sunlight, Dartmoor National Park.*

*The spectacular White Lady Falls, Lydford Gorge, Dartmoor National Park.*

*Wild flowers growing in the Valley of the Rocks, Exmoor National Park.*

*The rocky mound of Hound Tor, Dartmoor National Park.*

*A carpet of wood sorrel in the woodlands around Becky Falls near Manaton, Dartmoor National Park.*

*A woodland stream at Heddon's Mouth, Exmoor National Park.*

*A dry-stone wall on farmland near Princetown, Dartmoor National Park.*
*Opposite: A young fern growing out of the side of a tree at Heddon's Mouth, Exmoor National Park.*

*Jagged cliffs at Heddon's Mouth Cove, Exmoor National Park.*

*Pebbles on the beach at Heddon's Mouth Cove, Exmoor National Park.*

*Conifer plantation at Bellever, near Postbridge, Dartmoor National Park.*
*Opposite: A sheep in Wistman's Wood, west of Postbridge, in Dartmoor National Park.*

*A 'letterbox' hidden on Bonehill Down near Widecombe in the Moor, Dartmoor National Park. Letterboxing – leaving messages for other walkers to find – is popular on Dartmoor.*

*A view across Porlock Bay from Hurlstone Point, Exmoor National Park.*

*Pennywort growing in a dry-stone wall near Tarr Steps, Exmoor National Park.*

*Exmoor ponies on the lower slopes of Dunkery Beacon, Exmoor National Park.*

*The harbour at Porlock Weir, near Porlock, Exmoor National Park.*

*Wild flowers growing on an old stone wall, Porlock Weir, Exmoor National Park.*

*Above and opposite: Foliage in Wistman's Wood, west of Postbridge, Dartmoor National Park.*

*The peaceful little village of Widecombe in the Moor, Dartmoor National Park.*

*Vixen Tor, south of Merrivale, Dartmoor National Park.*

*Wood sorrell growing in Wistman's Wood, west of Postbridge, Dartmoor National Park.*
*Opposite: Wheal Betsy Tin Mine, Dartmoor National Park.*

*Stop for a cream tea at this well-kept thatched cottage in Selworthy, near Minehead, Exmoor National Park.*

*Some of the supporting buttresses on Tarr Steps, an ancient bridge across the River Barle near Dulverton, Exmoor National Park.*

*A rocky outcrop near Lynton separating the sea cliff from the Valley of the Rocks on the right, Exmoor National Park.*

*Castle Rock at the Valley of the Rocks near Lynton, Exmoor National Park.*

*Heather in flower on the slopes of Dunkery Beacon, Exmoor National Park.*

*The foamy waters of the rapids at Watersmeet near Lynmouth, Exmoor National Park.*

*A coastline view from the summit of the Valley of the Rocks near Lynton, Exmoor National Park.*

*Old oak woodland at Watersmeet near Lynmouth, Exmoor National Park.*

*Dawn at Scorhill Stone Circle near the village of Chagford, Dartmoor National Park.*

*Raised trackways, known as reaves, on Hamel Down near Grimspound in Dartmoor National Park.*

*North Teign River, Scorhill Down near Chagford, Dartmoor National Park.*

*The River Dart near Buckland in the Moor, Dartmoor National Park.*

*Clapper Bridge over the East Dart River near Postbridge, Dartmoor National Park.*

*The rushing waters of the waterfall at Watersmeet near Lynmouth, Exmoor National Park.*

*Foxgloves in flower on the path from Bossington to Hurlstone*
*Point, Exmoor National Park.*
*Opposite: Selworthy village nestles among the green folds of Exmoor National Park.*

*Gorse in flower on the slopes of Dunkery Beacon, Exmoor National Park.*

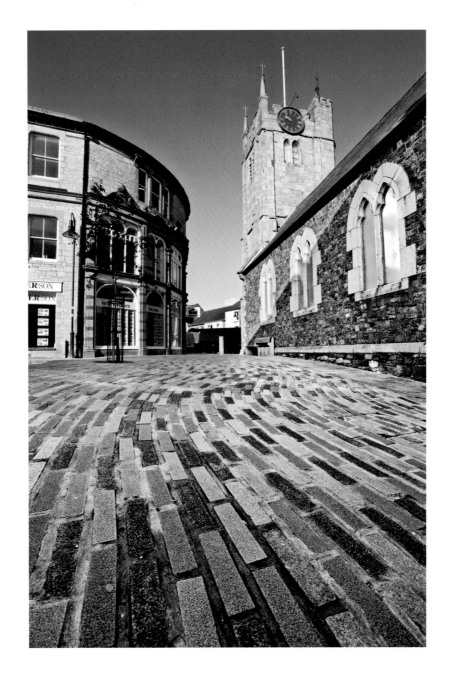

*Okehampton town centre, just outside Dartmoor National Park.*

*The remains of a Bronze Age settlement enclosed by a wall in Grimspound, Dartmoor National Park.*

*Letterboxing – leaving messages for other walkers to find – is popular on Dartmoor.*
*This box was found at Bonehill Down near Widecombe in the Moor.*

*A pony guards the Bronze Age ruins at Grimspound, Dartmoor National Park.*
*Opposite: A view across heather towards the Bristol Channel from Dunkery Beacon, Exmoor National Park.*

*A cairn on the summit of Dunkery Beacon, Exmoor National Park.*

*Thatched cottages in the picture-book village of Lustleigh, Dartmoor National Park.*

*Castle Rock at sunset, Valley of the Rocks, Lynton, Exmoor National Park.*

*The Dartmoor pony is a particularly hardy breed.*

*Consulting the map on Combestone Tor near Hexworthy, Dartmoor National Park.*
*Opposite: St Peter's Church in Buckland in the Moor, Dartmoor National Park.*

*The clock on St Peter's Church in Buckland in the Moor, Dartmoor National Park.*
*Opposite: Thatched cottages in the village of Buckland in the Moor, Dartmoor National Park.*

*Bowerman's Nose at Hayne Down near the village of Manaton,*
*Dartmoor National Park.*

*St Peter's Church in Buckland in the Moor, Dartmoor National Park.*

*A cabbage white butterfly perches on a flower at Manaton, Dartmoor National Park.*

*A rugged-looking Exmoor pony.*

# INDEX